Blood

poems by

Alana Dagenhart Sherrill

Finishing Line Press
Georgetown, Kentucky

Blood

ACKNOWLEDGMENTS

I am grateful to the editors of the following publications where these poems
appeared in slightly different versions:

Emrys: "Muscadines"
When Women Waken: "Study in Sorrow"

Blood could not have been written without the support and
encouragement of all my teachers and friends on the mountain at Wildacres
and my writing groups: Dede Mitchell and Amanda Winar, and SFD: Joyce
Compton Brown, Les Brown, and Thomas
Alexander.

Many thanks to Gretchen Dagenhart Sherrill for late-night writing
camaraderie and relentless editing, and to John Sherrill—thank you for
sharing your precious family with me.

To my parents, Tony and Diana Dagenhart—thank you for teaching me to
value little details and every single voice: I'm still listening.

Editor: Christen Kincaid

Cover Art and Design: Alana Dagenhart Sherrill

Author Photo: Georgia Marie Sherrill

Printed in the USA on acid-free paper.
Order online: www.finishinglinepress.com
              also available on amazon.com

Author inquiries and mail orders:
Finishing Line Press
P. O. Box 1626
Georgetown, Kentucky 40324
U. S. A.

Table of Contents

*For my children, Sidney, Gretchen, Davis, and Georgia
and in memory of my grandparents, Clyde, Marie, Glenn, Vera,
and Cat*

CADAVER

Watching the chest for rise and fall
I take his pulse, his heart refuses to quit
after he stops breathing his pulsing
pattern stubbornly beats

vainly, I memorize the moment
it replays in vivid detail
his face, the gnawed skin
drawn over slim sharp cheek bones

yellow teeth and hands
long skinny fingers
nicotine tinged nails, translucent crepe
bulging with green veins

hands that always offer me a twenty
for gas, or to vacuum
hands that for thirty six years will grip
the wheel of a Greyhound

shoo-off winos
on the night run from Charlotte to Atlanta
hands that load my bag
drive the miles

to Alaska and back
waving at truckers
through canyon lands
cafeterias, South Dakota

with DNR signed
I watch the dismantling of man
I hold his mortal hand
and kiss him

I look for a spirit rising
for something to dissipate
in air, for chrome flashes
but there is only silence.

CAT'S TOMATO BISCUITS

½ c. Crisco
½ c. buttermilk
Flour
Roll out dough. Dash salt. Use a juice jar to cut into tiny biscuits.
Don't let them burn. Add mayonnaise, a sliced tomato, salt &
pepper.

HOOPS

Before the first girl before whiskers
whiskey and puking
before too much disappointment
beyond a bad grade
while new Air Jordans can still change a life;
the bleached shell necklaces spar for manhood

they dance back and forth below a halo of nylon net
stars under one single amber lamppost
a circle of half-court shadows tomorrow
tonight they fly in the light
their bird chests glisten in sweat

Who's your papa?
Call me Daddy now
shooting insults through hoops
with grin and swish
pushing the ball into concrete
expecting it to return

I'VE GOT A BROTHER NAMED MATTHEW

no one knows
at least I think that's what they would've named him
I was whisked off to play with cousins
while my mother's uterus
was scraped out with a spoon
I don't know why we don't have him
I never thought to ask
it doesn't bother me much, but Dad
has tears in his eyes
I wished for more brothers
it would be nice now
maybe he would live close to me
our kids would play
maybe he and Josh would
work together

ALL MY DOGS

Everywhere I moved she was there
> He stole cartons from the truck, drank milk in the parking
> lot.

waiting to see what I would do next
> He licked my skinned knees.

waiting to see if I needed her
> She listened to my drama for hours in the barn.

and of course I always do
> She waited by the mailbox for my bus.

need her touch, her head bumping against my thigh
> She was my date every night after the breakup.

the soft baby fur of her chin on my foot
> She spoke, almost whinnied; when we talked.

as she lies by my chair on the porch.
> He was the soul of the unborn child, incarnate at my feet.

What did I ever do to deserve such devotion
> She barked until I found the copperhead
> by the toddler's sandbox.

not known to humans,
> She slept in his spot to keep me company when he was
> gone.

given this whole life;
> She licked my leg as I screamed and shook the thing—
> chewed.

the pure soul and deep eye
> On Christmas morning, he came back with half an ear.

that reads my mind
> His breathing slowed, his eyes fixed. I knew he was lost.

and fills my heart with joy?
> With every shovel stick and stomp I sobbed
> knowing it was good.

OLD SALEM, EASTER

We walk silently in the cold dark
listening for echoes
of brass trombones
among twittering birds

the mass shuffles
along in half-light
plodding toward the grave
between birth and death

there is equality in dirt

we stand at dawn
in God's Acre
she punches me when orange fire
reaches over the edge of the hill

the hair of the baby
in front of me turns
into a downy halo.
He squints; each white square

begins to glow electric
azalea magenta, forsythia
early green newborn leaves
the fresh pink of years.

DAUGHTER

I slide my hips onto the bed.

My daughter
what? fifty now?
smiles her hazel eyes
I apologize for urine stench

how did she get here?
She brushes the hair out of my eyes.
Yesterday I ran the trail
through the woods around the lake.

I need her
for time wrinkles
ripples, crashes.

She got out of the car at the ball field
rushed, ready to pitch
I'd washed the white pants
over and over again stained still with red clay

I fix her pony tail
kiss the sweat from her brow
it tastes of her: sun, rubies, and gold;

of tears that will fall slow down
in the night without memory
poetry-like.

ENLIGHTENMENT

It was February, your sophomore year
my spring break
I'd missed your voice

drove in grooves of ice behind salt trucks
three hours to you my brother
new stranger with your own world

edged off from this dungeon
away from mom's glare we stole cafeteria trays
for sledding snow drifts in winter's moon

your dingy apartment
those girls next door gave lessons
on how to drop acid

they had that poster on the dank
paneled wall where Ophelia floats
eternally in a pool of flowers

her eyes open
but she's dead right? Her eyes open
her hair

flowing from her head
rusting algae
her taffeta brocade skirts surfacing

you swept from room to room
drunk in love of names
and chartreuse sculptures of lichens

it began then, I guess
how you changed your mind
rejected us after that

how you stayed
on the mountain in that cinder block slum
which was more welcoming than home.

THE GARDENER

In the rose garden spraying for aphids
and Japanese beetles
her calloused hands' cultivate

faded pink polo
black knit pants
dirty tennis shoes

pale next to that
ravishing beaut
Mr. Lincoln

I see her and think of spring
how tender tendrils
reach up like children

delicate daffodils, spirea, forsythia
crowd around and scream
we're back

dogwood, azalea, redbud, fiery maple
Daddy's apple tree
bulge and show

turning their faces toward the sun
anxiously glancing back at her
—waiting for approval.

HE MIGHT AS WELL HAVE BEEN DAVID

His marble body:
curving calcite
fast twitch muscle fibers
set to spring or sprint
kinetic gastrocnemius
exploding into rock hard thighs
a distinct division of quadriceps
rivaling sculpture
the muscles, building form
then tapering
at superior ends joining sartorius
his lower torso
in chiseled triangulation
his smooth
adept hands exquisite
able hands ending in wide
symmetrical fingernails
incarnate later
on the hands of our daughter
I was useless
gone
taken
to his sassy
contrapposto swagger
and sad eyes
saying
hey baby

APRIL, 2009
for Samuel

Happy Birthday
baby sweet sapling
angel hair black
eleven in heaven
baby oak cut down
too soon

who knew?

who knew?

you came before
full-grown leaves
before
we knew the meaning
of *cerclage*
before
your papa could plane
a cherry cradle
before
your mama
knew to lie down

family of four
missing
one
baby oak
cut down
too
soon

THE PHOTOGRAPH

We stand smiling in long September
gold ochre shadows
on pastoral farmland
where Union soldiers slept
in early 1865

her hair ripples
in chestnut ringlets
falling on the boy's plaid shoulder
his arm squeezes his sister too tight

porch boards squeak with the weight
of so many
kids grown into parents
cut hay reminds us of afternoon heat
flashes of lightening bugs
his whistle calling us back
to the house for supper

no one speaks of yesterday's suspension
the heart attack
tumors
agitated alliances
or the push and pull of long marriage

truces drawn, we are civil
laughing in sunlight

CONVERSATIONS WITH CATHERINE

Hey Lana, she says in a sweet familiar voice of a friend my age
but she isn't my age, she's forty five, maybe more, years older
she knows me—I'm not sure how; maybe we are all the same
maybe I remind her of herself
maybe I am just every young mother.
She sees my face and tells me I look tired.

How many years do you have left?
Ten, she said. Maybe ten.
Is that all? I ask in disbelief
My body is giving out, Lana.
Oh. I'm sorry, I said.

She is right.

Getting old isn't so golden you know, she said.
There are lots of funerals.

You know you didn't bother me when you and Chub
came after Sidney was born and you made us pork tenderloin.
I know we bothered you. You didn't need our help.
Yes I did, I said. I can't make pork tenderloin.

OUR DEAD PUPPY

Our dead puppy
God's tiny creation
artificially warmed
by fervent rubbing
sleeps under poplars
in the side yard.

IT'S OVER

Their childhood
is spent.

How sinful
self centered
of me
to not have
cherished
every
precious day

to worry and
fly about
concerned with
time and
money and
laugh lines

absolute travesty

that I
slept or
worked or
read or
did

anything but
love

BODY GARDEN

At seven
on the summer
solstice of my
thirty seventh year

I saw long
shadows on the
stones
of Mary and John Sutton

stood over
some Susanna's
sod space

stood under
enormous
coniferous
Mr. Pon's Biology 101
flashes back
Ginkgo, Oak, Ailanthus' compound leaves,
Quercus palustris,
Fourth Creek Cemetery:
baby trees and babies too
blooming before their time

planted by family
genus
species
planted by family
during winter
during war
during harvest
planted

at seven on the
summer solstice I
snapped

self portraits
with
my dog.

STUDY IN SORROW

June

He'd died
so I watered the garden
counted stars
and tried to name constellations.
I listened for wind
and petted the calf.

Nothing happened
no one spoke
the bird girl wouldn't blink.

October

I think I must be falling apart
my hands dialed the number they know
the order of digits
it's muscle memory now
one day when the number slips away
my fingers will still remember

at midnight, I expect him to answer
that maybe it was all unreal
I'd been mistaken and he had come home
escaped the hospital when I wasn't there
snuck out or something, got a milkshake
and headed to the house

maybe he'd been there all summer
padding the floors, drinking coffee
watching David Letterman, waiting on me to call
I imagined the rotary phone in the little hallway
the notes with his scribbled text
the way the phone shook when it rang

I can't believe he would sit there and talk
to me all night like he did
—tied to that chair by the cord
where he couldn't even see the T.V.

March

I got up the last of the leaves by the patio and can't stop crying
it's funny how leaves and a garbage bag conjure the wailing

I bet the camellias are blooming in his side yard
with leaves underneath that spent the summer
above an empty house
then fell silently in October at four a.m.
with no one to see them while he no longer smoked in the driveway
waiting for the morning paper

leaves rotting by the fading white-washed gate
whose infancy paralleled false hopes
and when full grown
shaded his lawn while he drew his last breath.

May

Dear Clyde,

Thank you for the money you gave me for graduate school.
I missed you at graduation—you would've hated it though
it was way too long, and those roads to Shelby are no good.
Anyway, I'm finished and will get a job.
You never denied me anything.

Love,
Alana

P.S. Your yard looks good. The lady that bought the house
keeps up the leaves and the crepe myrtle has lots of buds.
She let me take a clipping of Emma's camellias to root.
I never thought I'd miss mowing.

MY SELF

has been taken
they won't give her back.
I've demanded to talk to her
they always give me the run around—
she's busy right now or
she just got in the shower
one day I'm going to sneak in
see if I can catch her before they stop me
catch up, have coffee

I can feel her sometimes
I check my texts and recheck
see if she's sent me a message

I know it is killing her
never a break
the running, the laundry, the algebra
and I'm like, Jesus, just let her be
you're working her to death
it does not matter if the corner drawer is cluttered
keep this up I say
she might become an alcoholic.
Nah. She thinks she's under control.

MOM AND MARIE

The lady that bought the house asks
Did she die here? and Mom said Yes
and followed with
She was the sweetest spirit I ever knew
which wasn't true at all
because everyone knew Mom hated Marie
loathed her even
but cherished somehow the final months
when she took care

of Marie's dying body, colostomy bag and all
because Mom just loves to be needed
loves to be in control and in charge
so naturally
when her mother-in-law's cancer metastasized
when cells went hog wild
they ignored their love-hate relationship.

Changing someone's colostomy bag, when someone
changes your colostomy bag
it makes up for years of bitterness
it's disgusting
it should be privately endured
but it couldn't and pride
becomes nonexistent
you get over the queasiness
the yuck factor

you do what you gotta do
and Marie's eyes eased on Mom
and neither of them ever wished
to be in these circumstances:
to be the shitter
and the shittee, yet it was that movement
of biological matter
that humbled them and let them love
the other enough.

DEAR NELL,

Thank you
because
they've buried you
before I knew you
were gone

Thank you
for knowing me for
not knowing me for
wishing I had all boys for
blue eyes for
sweet smile for
stubborn perseverance for
help dragging the
deer to the truck for
being funny for
all the invitations
I never accepted
Thank you, dear Nell

REALITY

I miss you with the weight of big water
sweet Catherine
that comes in the night
don't you remember?
with sobbing
and uncontrollable shudders
I cannot believe you are gone

sometimes I feel like you called
I hear your voice
you left a message
one day I'll come home to find a bowl
of fresh cooked collards
or a pan of stickies
on my porch—straight from your kitchen.

HERE AFTER

When I am dead come see me
in the ripple of the water
in the space between waves

in the moon cycle
like a circle
like a smile behind green swirls

in the swerve and the whirl of the eddy
in the stream of speckled trout
in the slave song dark as Dismal

come swim or paddle out to Pamlico warm.

With cypress hair
and tannin blood I'm here
in the entranced lake

where meteors flash
across a black iron glass of stillness

in the mystic fairy land
of enchanted mill ponds
I'll wait for you among the knees

hang your candle in a tree
so that you can find the shore

when your kayak slices the water
I'll know it's you.

MUSCADINES

The yard, a snarled profile
of what used to be when she tended the space
before kudzu crowded her brain
and she went all savage
we pinched mums, pruned crepe myrtles
picked up persimmons for pudding

the grapes shriveled up, sucked dry
like old hands
or dead spiders
remind me of the vine in the back
up the hill in the only space of long sun
overgrown now with weeds

we'd nestle under the pergola
sit in cool dirt skirted leaves
with stories
the thriving lush smelled thick
so distinctly of this place
the taste of muscadine wine

flashbacks up vertebrae to resonate
in the middle of a silver screen
that plays large and bright
on the edge of town
just out of earshot
where actors move about
their voices—musky sweet in July—
rise up off pavement in wavy laughter

NOW

Today is calm, fine. They all went to school. I took a nap. The meat is on the counter for supper. I made a list for the store, started laundry, emptied trash, fed the dog. She is on the porch—her paws just so. Her charcoal coat glistens like taffeta; dark in places and shiny here and occasionally iridescent. The bee buzzes at the screen looking for a way out. Birds flit and chirp in the yard, the air is still and cool. The wood floor is sure. The cardinal crosses the yard, his head this way and that, cocked and jerked as he hops from blade to blade. Right now we are fine. Not far off the jet engine breaks the silence. Noise crowds the air, reminds me of bombs, not far off. Bombs that drop one day in September, out of the blue, or maybe April, at the end of a marathon. Bombs that will blare, wail, gash, and lacerate lives like Dad's buckshot tumors in February and we will stitch patch the place back together, but it won't be the same. We will say we are good, we are strong, we can endure, not believing we will. But today; practice softball, study physics, mail the gas bill, sweep the kitchen, get eggs and liver mush. The rooster crows just across the fence, dragonflies carve rough figure eights in noon light, and dandelions litter the lawn while dishes stack in my sink.

THE FIRST GRADER'S HANDWRITING

His name, carefully printed
in large block letters
on the pull-out top of the tiny desk
memorialize his life as artifact

proof that he actually existed
because he hadn't accumulated much
by that seventh summer
when his bike rumpled under a bumper

after that, how items became precious
the one school picture in his horn-rimmed glasses
the leather bomber jacket
the die-cast Chevy truck with running boards

His dog would die years later
the last scrap of his little life
we clung to like he did to breath
those ten short days in July

BEFORE YOUR LEAVING

"The body, lady, is like a house; it don't go anywhere; but the spirit, lady, is like an automobile: Always on the move, always . . ."
~ Flannery O'Connor in "The Life you Save May be Your Own."

I thought about you in your infancy
how your skin might have looked
all wrinkly and golden
not unlike your hands at the end
when I could see through translucence to green veins

how you smelled before decades
behind the dash of a Greyhound
and the look in your mother's eyes when she saw you
you must have been a sight
I wonder did she cringe at the thought of another child
the forth of nine she would birth
wasn't she tired already?

and you
hard-wired for humor and easy
who would know your life?
how maps and old men in overalls
would change you—how you were no farm boy
but born for city, arriving for roads
needing street lights neon people
four a.m. and newspapers in driveways

the baby fast-forward
to school to girls to cigarettes stuffed in pockets
ditching the car
failing chemistry learning Latin
and somehow you understood physics
then tanks in Italy and a stolen Fiat
arrivederci you said *arrivederci*

then a girl from the mill with a marriage license
from the Yorktown Justice of the Peace
a quick newborn boy with your skin and the same eyes blinking
blinking starting to wail but even he
wouldn't keep you home
very long

Alana Dagenhart Sherrill is a poet, artist, and scholar from North Carolina. Her poems have been published in several journals including *Emrys, Main Street Rag, When Women Waken,* and *Pinesong.* She won the Caldwell Nixon, Jr. Contest from the North Carolina Poetry Society, served as a panelist on "Poetry of Place" in Carboro's Westend Poetry Festival, and read her poem "The Road" on WUNC's "The State of Things" with Frank Stasio. Her most recent scholarship focuses on poetry of the southern Appalachian Mountains.

She is an assistant professor of English at Johnson & Wales University in Charlotte, serves as a volunteer for the Iredell Arts Council, and the New South Gallery & Studios, where she hosts a monthly open-mic night. She spends her free time watching the stars (especially over Manteo), learning the banjo, and snowboarding. She lives mostly in Statesville and sometimes, Boone.